C000127579

Wessex

Wessex Poems

Thomas Hardy

ET REMOTISSIMA PROPE

Hesperus Poetry

Hesperus Poetry
Published by Hesperus Press Limited
4 Rickett Street, London SW6 1RU
www.hesperuspress.com

First published in 1898
First published by Hesperus Press Limited, 2007

Designed and typeset by Fraser Muggeridge studio
Printed in Jordan by Jordan National Press

Foreword © Tom Paulin, 2007

ISBN: 1-84391-148-5
ISBN13: 978-1-84391-148-7

All rights reserved. This book is sold subject to the condition that it shall not be resold, lent, hired out or otherwise circulated without the express prior consent of the publisher.

CONTENTS

FOREWORD

In 1898, Hardy published *Wessex Poems* and retired from novel-writing. He was fifty-eight years old, and had been bruised by the reception of *Tess of the D'Urbervilles* and *Jude the Obscure*, but poetry had been his first love and now he returned to it, collecting new and early poems in the volume. Though it had a print run of only 500 copies, *Wessex Poems* was widely reviewed, and Hardy took some of the criticisms to heart. Towards the end of his life, in his disguised autobiography he reflected on the critical reception of the volume.

In the reception of this and later volumes of Hardy's poems there was, he said, as regards form, the inevitable ascription to ignorance of what was really choice after full knowledge. That the author loved the art of concealing art was undiscerned – for instance, as to rhythm. Years earlier he had decided that too regular a beat was bad art. He had fortified himself in his opinion by thinking of the analogy of architecture, between which art and that of poetry he had discovered, to use his own words, that there existed a close and curious parallel – both arts, unlike some others, having to carry a rational content inside their artistic form. He knew that in architecture cunning irregularity is of enormous worth, and it is obvious that he carried on into his verse, perhaps in part unconsciously, the Gothic art principle in which he had been trained – the principle of spontaneity, found in mouldings, tracery, and such like – resulting in the 'unforeseen' (as it has been called) character of his metres and stanzas, that of stress rather than of syllable, poetic texture rather than poetic veneer; the latter kind of thing, under the name of 'constructed ornament', being what he, in common with every Gothic student, had been taught to avoid as the plague. He shaped his poetry accordingly, introducing metrical pauses and reversed beats, and found for his trouble that some particular line exemplifying this principle was greeted with a would-be jocular remark that such a line 'did not make for immortality'. The same critic might have gone to one of our cathedrals (to follow up the analogy of architecture), and on discovering that the carved leafage of some capital or spandrel in the best period of Gothic art strayed freakishly out of its bounds over the moulding, where by rule it had no business to be, or that the enrichments of a string-course were not accurately spaced, or that there was a sudden blank in a wall where a window was expected from formal measurement, have declared with equally merry conviction, 'This does not make for immortality'.

This is the most extensive statement of the Gothic principle that underlies all Hardy's writing, and it shows how his work is grounded in his early career as an architect and in his reading of Ruskin on the nature of Gothic. We can see it at work in 'The Ivy-Wife', which begins with a song-like clarity:

I longed to love a full-boughed beech
　　And be as high as he:
I stretched an arm within his reach,
　　And signalled unity.
But with his drip he forced a breach,
　　And tried to poison me.

Then at the end Hardy crams stresses together:

　　Soon he,
Being bark-bound, flagged, snapped, fell outright,
　　And in his fall felled me!

The impacted, textured quality of 'Being bark-bound, flagged, snapped, fell outright' is Gothic.

The first edition of *Wessex Poems* is remarkable for Hardy's illustrations, and the image he gives for 'In a Eweleaze Near Weatherbury' is extraordinary, surreal, as we see a pair of wire-rimmed spectacles sitting on the landscape as on a desk. This is Hardy's poetry of perception, his constant preoccupation with gazing eyes, as well as his theme of youth and age.

Many of the poems in this collection were written in his early twenties and they show the influence of Shakespeare's sonnets, Meredith's *Modern Love*, Browning and Tennyson. The, as he called it, 'dramatic or personative' nature of many of the poems shows the influence of Browning, to whose poems he was devoted. But early in the collection we hear Hardy's distinctive voice in 'Neutral Tones':

> *We stood by a pond that winter day,*
> *And the sun was white, as though chidden of God,*
> *And a few leaves lay on the starving sod,*
>   *– They had fallen from an ash, and were gray.*

This is Arnold's darkling plain, the universe post-Darwin. We catch the distinctive speaking voice that shapes Hardy's best poems in that apparently extemporised fourth line, and though the next two stanzas fall away from the opening this delineating spontaneity is recuperated powerfully in the last stanza:

> *Since then, keen lessons that love deceives,*
> *And wrings with wrong, have shaped to me*
> *Your face, and the God-curst sun, and a tree,*
>   *And a pond edged with grayish leaves.*

The subtle speaking voice that plays against normative metre and which is such a crucial part of Hardy's Gothic aesthetic can be heard in the opening lines of 'Friends Beyond', which like so many of his poems is set in a graveyard:

> *William Dewy, Tranter Reuben, Farmer Ledlow late*
> > *at plough,*
> > *Robert's kin, and John's, and Ned's,*
> *And the Squire, and Lady Susan, lie in Mellstock*
> > *churchyard now!*

The way Hardy shifts from trochaics to iambic metre in 'and John's, and Ned's' shows that patient voice at work.

That voice is grounded in Dorset speech and folk song – many of the poems are in ballad form, and often they are about the Napoleonic Wars, and so look forward to Hardy's unread epic *The Dynasts*. He also draws on Dorset dialect, whose use he justifies in the preface, saying that whenever an 'ancient and legitimate word of the district, for which there was no equivalent in received English' suggested itself he included it. His collection is a notable expression of his folkloric imagination and needs to be read outside the collected poems, as he first intended it should be. Like the architect in 'Heiress and Architect' he is a man of 'measuring eye', but he is also fascinated by the uniqueness of individual voices. *Wessex Poems* is brimful of characters, each with their own distinctive voice.

– *Tom Paulin, 2007*

PREFACE

Of the miscellaneous collection of verse that follows, only four pieces have been published, though many were written long ago, and others partly written. In some few cases the verses were turned into prose and printed as such, it having been unanticipated at that time that they might see the light.

Whenever an ancient and legitimate word of the district, for which there was no equivalent in received English, suggested itself as the most natural, nearest, and often only expression of a thought, it has been made use of, on what seemed good grounds.

The pieces are in a large degree dramatic or personative in conception, and this even where they are not obviously so.

The dates attached to some of the poems do not apply to the rough sketches given in illustration, which have been recently made, and, as may be surmised, are inserted for personal and local reasons rather than for their intrinsic qualities.

– T.H., September 1898

Wessex Poems

And Other Verses

The Temporary The All

Change and chancefulness in my flowering youthtime,
Set me sun by sun near to one unchosen;
Wrought us fellow-like, and despite divergence,
Friends interlinked us.

'Cherish him can I while the true one forthcome –
Come the rich fulfiller of my prevision;
Life is roomy yet, and the odds unbounded.'
So self-communed I.

Thwart my wistful way did a damsel saunter,
Fair, the while unformed to be all-eclipsing;
'Maiden meet,' held I, 'till arise my forefelt
Wonder of women.'

Long a visioned hermitage deep desiring,
Tenements uncouth I was fain to house in;
'Let such lodging be for a breath-while,' thought I,
'Soon a more seemly.

'Then, high handiwork will I make my life-deed,
Truth and Light outshow; but the ripe time pending,
Intermissive aim at the thing sufficeth.'
Thus I... But lo, me!

Mistress, friend, place, aims to be bettered straightway,
Bettered not has Fate or my hand's achieving;
Sole the showance those of my onward earth-track –
Never transcended!

Amabel

I marked her ruined hues,
Her custom-straitened views,
And asked, 'Can there indwell
   My Amabel?'

I looked upon her gown,
Once rose, now earthen brown;
The change was like the knell
   Of Amabel.

Her step's mechanic ways
Had lost the life of May's;
Her laugh, once sweet in swell,
   Spoilt Amabel.

I mused: 'Who sings the strain
I sang ere warmth did wane?
Who thinks its numbers spell
   His Amabel?' –

Knowing that, though Love cease,
Love's race shows undecrease;
All find in dorp or dell
   An Amabel.

– I felt that I could creep
To some housetop, and weep,
That Time the tyrant fell
   Ruled Amabel!

I said (the while I sighed
That love like ours had died),
'Fond things I'll no more tell
    To Amabel,

'But leave her to her fate,
And fling across the gate,
"Till the Last Trump, farewell,
    O Amabel!"'

1865

Hap

If but some vengeful god would call to me
From up the sky, and laugh: 'Thou suffering thing,
Know that thy sorrow is my ecstasy,
That thy love's loss is my hate's profiting!'

Then would I bear, and clench myself, and die,
Steeled by the sense of ire unmerited;
Half-eased in that a Powerfuller than I
Had willed and meted me the tears I shed.

But not so. How arrives it joy lies slain,
And why unblooms the best hope ever sown?
– Crass Casualty obstructs the sun and rain,
And dicing Time for gladness casts a moan…
These purblind Doomsters had as readily strown
Blisses about my pilgrimage as pain.

1866

'In Vision I Roamed'
To —

In vision I roamed the flashing Firmament,
So fierce in blazon that the Night waxed wan,
As though with an awed sense of such ostent;
And as I thought my spirit ranged on and on

In footless traverse through ghast heights of sky,
To the last chambers of the monstrous Dome,
Where stars the brightest here to darkness die:
Then, any spot on our own Earth seemed Home!

And the sick grief that you were far away
Grew pleasant thankfulness that you were near,
Who might have been, set on some outstep sphere,
Less than a Want to me, as day by day
I lived unware, uncaring all that lay
Locked in that Universe taciturn and drear.

1866

At a Bridal
To —

When you paced forth, to wait maternity,
A dream of other offspring held my mind,
Compounded of us twain as Love designed;
Rare forms, that corporate now will never be!

Should I, too, wed as slave to Mode's decree,
And each thus found apart, of false desire,
A stolid line, whom no high aims will fire
As had fired ours could ever have mingled we;

And, grieved that lives so matched should mis-compose,
Each mourn the double waste; and question dare
To the Great Dame whence incarnation flows,
Why those high-purposed children never were:
What will she answer? That she does not care
If the race all such sovereign types unknows.

1866

Postponement

Snow-bound in woodland, a mournful word,
Dropt now and then from the bill of a bird,
Reached me on wind-wafts; and thus I heard,
   Wearily waiting: –

'I planned her a nest in a leafless tree,
But the passers eyed and twitted me,
And said: "How reckless a bird is he,
   Cheerily mating!"

'Fear-filled, I stayed me till summer-tide,
In lewth of leaves to throne her bride;
But alas! her love for me waned and died,
   Wearily waiting.

'Ah, had I been like some I see,
Born to an evergreen nesting-tree,
None had eyed and twitted me,
   Cheerily mating!'

1866

A Confession to a Friend in Trouble

Your troubles shrink not, though I feel them less
Here, far away, than when I tarried near;
I even smile old smiles – with listlessness –
Yet smiles they are, not ghastly mockeries mere.

A thought too strange to house within my brain
Haunting its outer precincts I discern:
– *That I will not show zeal again to learn*
Your griefs, and sharing them, renew my pain...

It goes, like murky bird or buccaneer
That shapes its lawless figure on the main,
And each new impulse tends to make outflee
The unseemly instinct that had lodgment here;
Yet, comrade old, can bitterer knowledge be
Than that, though banned, such instinct was in me!

1866

Neutral Tones

We stood by a pond that winter day,
And the sun was white, as though chidden of God,
And a few leaves lay on the starving sod,
   – They had fallen from an ash, and were gray.

Your eyes on me were as eyes that rove
Over tedious riddles solved years ago;
And some words played between us to and fro –
   On which lost the more by our love.

The smile on your mouth was the deadest thing
Alive enough to have strength to die;
And a grin of bitterness swept thereby
   Like an ominous bird a-wing…

Since then, keen lessons that love deceives,
And wrings with wrong, have shaped to me
Your face, and the God-curst sun, and a tree,
   And a pond edged with grayish leaves.

1867

She
At His Funeral

They bear him to his resting-place –
In slow procession sweeping by;
I follow at a stranger's space;
His kindred they, his sweetheart I.
Unchanged my gown of garish dye,
Though sable-sad is their attire;
But they stand round with griefless eye,
Whilst my regret consumes like fire!

187–

Her Initials

Upon a poet's page I wrote
Of old two letters of her name;
Part seemed she of the effulgent thought
Whence that high singer's rapture came.
– When now I turn the leaf the same
Immortal light illumes the lay,
But from the letters of her name
The radiance has died away!

1869

Her Dilemma
(In — Church)

The two were silent in a sunless church,
Whose mildewed walls, uneven paving-stones,
And wasted carvings passed antique research;
And nothing broke the clock's dull monotones.

Leaning against a wormy poppy-head,
So wan and worn that he could scarcely stand,
– For he was soon to die, – he softly said,
'Tell me you love me!' – holding hard her hand.

She would have given a world to breathe 'yes' truly,
So much his life seemed hanging on her mind,
And hence she lied, her heart persuaded throughly
'Twas worth her soul to be a moment kind.

But the sad need thereof, his nearing death,
So mocked humanity that she shamed to prize
A world conditioned thus, or care for breath
Where Nature such dilemmas could devise.

1866

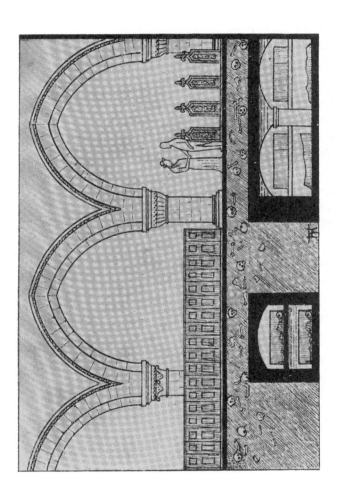

Revulsion

Though I waste watches framing words to fetter
Some spirit to mine own in clasp and kiss,
Out of the night there looms a sense 'twere better
To fail obtaining whom one fails to miss.

For winning love we win the risk of losing,
And losing love is as one's life were riven;
It cuts like contumely and keen ill-using
To cede what was superfluously given.

Let me then feel no more the fateful thrilling
That devastates the love-worn wooer's frame,
The hot ado of fevered hopes, the chilling
That agonises disappointed aim!
So may I live no junctive law fulfilling,
And my heart's table bear no woman's name.

1866

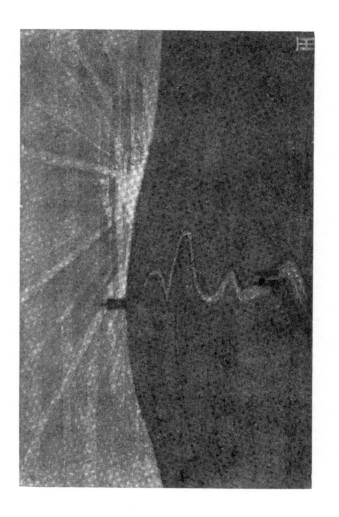

She, to Him

I

When you shall see me in the toils of Time,
My lauded beauties carried off from me,
My eyes no longer stars as in their prime,
My name forgot of Maiden Fair and Free;

When in your being heart concedes to mind,
And judgment, though you scarce its process know,
Recalls the excellencies I once enshrined,
And you are irked that they have withered so:

Remembering that with me lies not the blame,
That Sportsman Time but rears his brood to kill,
Knowing me in my soul the very same –
One who would die to spare you touch of ill! –
Will you not grant to old affection's claim
The hand of friendship down Life's sunless hill?

1866

She, to Him
II

Perhaps, long hence, when I have passed away,
Some other's feature, accent, thought like mine,
Will carry you back to what I used to say,
And bring some memory of your love's decline.

Then you may pause awhile and think, 'Poor jade!'
And yield a sigh to me – as ample due,
Not as the tittle of a debt unpaid
To one who could resign her all to you –

And thus reflecting, you will never see
That your thin thought, in two small words conveyed,
Was no such fleeting phantom-thought to me,
But the Whole Life wherein my part was played;
And you amid its fitful masquerade
A Thought – as I in yours but seem to be.

1866

She, to Him
III

I will be faithful to thee; aye, I will!
And Death shall choose me with a wondering eye
That he did not discern and domicile
One his by right ever since that last Good-bye!

I have no care for friends, or kin, or prime
Of manhood who deal gently with me here;
Amid the happy people of my time
Who work their love's fulfilment, I appear

Numb as a vane that cankers on its point,
True to the wind that kissed ere canker came;
Despised by souls of Now, who would disjoint
The mind from memory, and make Life all aim,

My old dexterities of hue quite gone,
And nothing left for Love to look upon.

1866

She, to Him
IV

This love puts all humanity from me;
I can but maledict her, pray her dead,
For giving love and getting love of thee –
Feeding a heart that else mine own had fed!

How much I love I know not, life not known,
Save as some unit I would add love by;
But this I know, my being is but thine own –
Fused from its separateness by ecstasy.

And thus I grasp thy amplitudes, of her
Ungrasped, though helped by nigh-regarding eyes;
Canst thou then hate me as an envier
Who see unrecked what I so dearly prize?
Believe me, Lost One, Love is lovelier
The more it shapes its moan in selfish-wise.

1866

Ditty
(E.L.G.)

Beneath a knap where flown
   Nestlings play,
Within walls of weathered stone,
   Far away
From the files of formal houses,
By the bough the firstling browses,
Lives a Sweet: no merchants meet,
No man barters, no man sells
   Where she dwells.

Upon that fabric fair
   'Here is she!'
Seems written everywhere
   Unto me.
But to friends and nodding neighbours,
Fellow-wights in lot and labours,
Who descry the times as I,
No such lucid legend tells
   Where she dwells.

Should I lapse to what I was
   Ere we met;
(Such can not be, but because
   Some forget
Let me feign it) – none would notice
That where she I know by rote is
Spread a strange and withering change,
Like a drying of the wells
   Where she dwells.

To feel I might have kissed –
    Loved as true –
Otherwhere, nor Mine have missed
    My life through,
Had I never wandered near her,
Is a smart severe – severer
In the thought that she is nought,
Even as I, beyond the dells
    Where she dwells.

And Devotion droops her glance
    To recall
What bond-servants of Chance
    We are all.
I but found her in that, going
On my errant path unknowing,
I did not out-skirt the spot
That no spot on earth excels,
    –Where she dwells!

1870

The Sergeant's Song
(1803)

When Lawyers strive to heal a breach,
And Parsons practise what they preach;
Then Little Boney[1] he'll pounce down,
And march his men on London town!
   Rollicum-rorum, tol-lol-lorum,
   Rollicum-rorum, tol-lol-lay!

When Justices hold equal scales,
And Rogues are only found in jails;
Then Little Boney he'll pounce down,
And march his men on London town!
   Rollicum-rorum, &c.

When Rich Men find their wealth a curse,
And fill therewith the Poor Man's purse;
Then Little Boney he'll pounce down,
And march his men on London town!
   Rollicum-rorum, &c.

When Husbands with their Wives agree,
And Maids won't wed from modesty;
Then Little Boney he'll pounce down,
And march his men on London town!
   Rollicum-rorum, tol-tol-lorum,
   Rollicum-rorum, tol-lol-lay!

1878

Published in *The Trumpet-Major*,[2] 1880

Valenciennes
(1793)

By Corp'l Tullidge: see *The Trumpet-Major*
In memory of S.C. (Pensioner). Died 184–

We trenched, we trumpeted and drummed,
And from our mortars tons of iron hummed
　　Ath'art the ditch, the month we bombed
　　　　The Town o' Valencieën.

'Twas in the June o' Ninety-dree
(The Duke o' Yark our then Commander beën)
　　The German Legion, Guards, and we
　　　　Laid siege to Valencieën.

This was the first time in the war
That French and English spilled each other's gore;
　　– Few dreamt how far would roll the roar
　　　　Begun at Valencieën!

'Twas said that we'd no business there
A-topperen the French for disagreën;
　　However, that's not my affair –
　　　　We were at Valencieën.

Such snocks and slats, since war began
Never knew raw recruit or veteran:
　　Stone-deaf therence went many a man
　　　　Who served at Valencieën.

Into the streets, ath'art the sky,
A hundred thousand balls and bombs were fleën;
  And harmless townsfolk fell to die
    Each hour at Valencieën!

And, sweaten wi' the bombardiers,
A shell was slent to shards anighst my ears:
  – 'Twas nigh the end of hopes and fears
    For me at Valencieën!

They bore my wownded frame to camp,
And shut my gapen skull, and washed en clean,
  And jined en wi' a zilver clamp
    Thik night at Valencieën.

'We've fetched en back to quick from dead;
But never more on earth while rose is red
  Will drum rouse Corpel!' Doctor said
    O' me at Valencieën.

'Twer true. No voice o' friend or foe
Can reach me now, or any liven beën;
  And little have I power to know
    Since then at Valencieën!

I never hear the zummer hums
O' bees; and don' know when the cuckoo comes;
  But night and day I hear the bombs
    We threw at Valencieën...

As for the Duke o' Yark in war,
There be some volk whose judgment o' en is meän;
    But this I say – a was not far
        From great at Valencieën.

O' wild wet nights, when all seems sad,
My wownds come back, as though new wownds I'd had;
    But yet – at times I'm sort o' glad
        I fout at Valencieën.

Well: Heaven wi' its jasper halls
Is now the on'y Town I care to be in…
    Good Lord, if Nick should bomb the walls
        As we did Valencieën!

1878–1897

San Sebastian
(August 1813)

With thoughts of Sergeant M— (Pensioner), who died 185–

'Why, Sergeant, stray on the Ivel Way,
As though at home there were spectres rife?
From first to last 'twas a proud career!
And your sunny years with a gracious wife
    Have brought you a daughter dear.

'I watched her to-day; a more comely maid,
As she danced in her muslin bowed with blue,
Round a Hintock maypole never gayed.'
– 'Aye, aye; I watched her this day, too,
    As it happens,' the Sergeant said.

'My daughter is now,' he again began,
'Of just such an age as one I knew
When we of the Line and Forlorn-hope van,
On an August morning – a chosen few –
    Stormed San Sebastian.

'She's a score less three; so about was *she* –
The maiden I wronged in Peninsular days...[3]
You may prate of your prowess in lusty times,
But as years gnaw inward you blink your bays,
    And see too well your crimes!

'We'd stormed it at night, by the vlanker-light
Of burning towers, and the mortar's boom:
We'd topped the breach; but had failed to stay,

For our files were misled by the baffling gloom;
   And we said we'd storm by day.

'So, out of the trenches, with features set,
On that hot, still morning, in measured pace,
Our column climbed; climbed higher yet,
Past the fauss'bray, scarp, up the curtain-face,
   And along the parapet.

'From the battened hornwork the cannoneers
Hove crashing balls of iron fire;
On the shaking gap mount the volunteers
In files, and as they mount expire
   Amid curses, groans, and cheers.

'Five hours did we storm, five hours re-form,
As Death cooled those hot blood pricked on;
Till our cause was helped by a woe within:
They swayed from the summit we'd leapt upon,
   And madly we entered in.

'On end for plunder, 'mid rain and thunder
That burst with the lull of our cannonade,
We vamped the streets in the stifling air –
Our hunger unsoothed, our thirst unstayed –
   And ransacked the buildings there.

'Down the stony steps of the house-fronts white
We rolled rich puncheons of Spanish grape,
Till at length, with the fire of the wine alight,
I saw at a doorway a fair fresh shape –
   A woman, a sylph, or sprite.

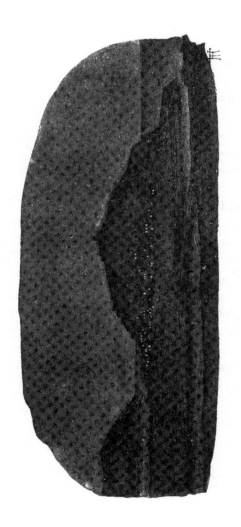

'Afeard she fled, and with heated head
I pursued to the chamber she called her own;
– When might is right no qualms deter,
And having her helpless and alone
   I wreaked my will on her.

'She raised her beseeching eyes to me,
And I heard the words of prayer she sent
In her own soft language… Seemingly
I copied those eyes for my punishment
   In begetting the girl you see!

'So, to-day I stand with a God-set brand
Like Cain's, when he wandered from kindred's ken…
I served through the war that made Europe free;
I wived me in peace-year. But, hid from men,
   I bear that mark on me.

'And I nightly stray on the Ivel Way
As though at home there were spectres rife;
I delight me not in my proud career;
And 'tis coals of fire that a gracious wife
   Should have brought me a daughter dear!'

The Stranger's Song

(As sung by Mr Charles Charrington in the play of *The Three Wayfarers*[4])

O my trade it is the rarest one,
    Simple shepherds all –
  My trade is a sight to see;
For my customers I tie, and take 'em up on high,
    And waft 'em to a far countree!

My tools are but common ones,
    Simple shepherds all –
  My tools are no sight to see:
A little hempen string, and a post whereon to swing,
    Are implements enough for me!

To-morrow is my working day,
    Simple shepherds all –
  To-morrow is a working day for me:
For the farmer's sheep is slain, and the lad who did it ta'en,
    And on his soul may God ha' mer-cy!

Printed in 'The Three Strangers',[5] 1883

The Burghers

(17–)

The sun had wheeled from Grey's to Dammer's Crest,
And still I mused on that Thing imminent:
At length I sought the High-street to the West.

The level flare raked pane and pediment
And my wrecked face, and shaped my nearing friend
Like one of those the Furnace held unshent.

'I've news concerning her,' he said. 'Attend.
They fly to-night at the late moon's first gleam:
Watch with thy steel: two righteous thrusts will end

Her shameless visions and his passioned dream.
I'll watch with thee, to testify thy wrong –
To aid, maybe. – Law consecrates the scheme.'

I started, and we paced the flags along
Till I replied: 'Since it has come to this
I'll do it! But alone. I can be strong.'

Three hours past Curfew, when the Froom's[6] mild
    hiss
Reigned sole, undulled by whirr of merchandise,
From Pummery-Tout to where the Gibbet is,

I crossed my pleasaunce hard by Glyd'path Rise,
And stood beneath the wall. Eleven strokes went,
And to the door they came, contrariwise,

And met in clasp so close I had but bent
My lifted blade upon them to have let
Their two souls loose upon the firmament.

But something held my arm. 'A moment yet
As pray-time ere you wantons die!' I said;
And then they saw me. Swift her gaze was set

With eye and cry of love illimited
Upon her Heart-king. Never upon me
Had she thrown look of love so thorough-sped!...

At once she flung her faint form shieldingly
On his, against the vengeance of my vows;
The which o'erruling, her shape shielded he.

Blanked by such love, I stood as in a drowse,
And the slow moon edged from the upland nigh,
My sad thoughts moving thuswise: 'I may house

And I may husband her, yet what am I
But licensed tyrant to this bonded pair?
Says Charity, Do as ye would be done by.'...

Hurling my iron to the bushes there,
I bade them stay. And, as if brain and breast
Were passive, they walked with me to the stair.

Inside the house none watched; and on we prest
Before a mirror, in whose gleam I read
Her beauty, his, – and mine own mien unblest;

Till at her room I turned. 'Madam,' I said,
'Have you the wherewithal for this? Pray speak.
Love fills no cupboard. You'll need daily bread.'

'We've nothing, sire,' said she; 'and nothing seek.
'Twere base in me to rob my lord unware;
Our hands will earn a pittance week by week.'

And next I saw she'd piled her raiment rare
Within the garde-robes, and her household purse,
Her jewels, and least lace of personal wear;

And stood in homespun. Now grown wholly hers,
I handed her the gold, her jewels all,
And him the choicest of her robes diverse.

'I'll take you to the doorway in the wall,
And then adieu,' I to them. 'Friends, withdraw.'
They did so; and she went – beyond recall.

And as I paused beneath the arch I saw
Their moonlit figures – slow, as in surprise –
Descend the slope, and vanish on the haw.

'"Fool," some will say,' I thought. 'But who is wise,
Save God alone, to weigh my reasons why?'
– 'Hast thou struck home?' came with the boughs'
    night-sighs.

It was my friend. 'I have struck well. They fly,
But carry wounds that none can cicatrise.'
– 'Not mortal?' said he. 'Lingering – worse,' said I.

Leipzig

(1813)

Scene: The Master-tradesmen's Parlour at the Old Ship Inn, Casterbridge. Evening.

'Old Norbert with the flat blue cap –
    A German said to be –
Why let your pipe die on your lap,
    Your eyes blink absently?' –

– 'Ah!... Well, I had thought till my cheek was wet
    Of my mother – her voice and mien
When she used to sing and pirouette,
    And touse the tambourine

'To the march that yon street-fiddler plies:
    She told me 'twas the same
She'd heard from the trumpets, when the Allies
    Her city overcame.

'My father was one of the German Hussars,
    My mother of Leipzig; but he,
Long quartered here, fetched her at close of the wars,
    And a Wessex lad reared me.

'And as I grew up, again and again
    She'd tell, after trilling that air,
Of her youth, and the battles on Leipzig plain
    And of all that was suffered there!...

' – 'Twas a time of alarms. Three Chiefs-at-arms
    Combined them to crush One,

And by numbers' might, for in equal fight
    He stood the matched of none.

'Carl Schwarzenberg was of the plot,
    And Blücher, prompt and prow,
And Jean the Crown-Prince Bernadotte:
    Buonaparte was the foe.

'City and plain had felt his reign
    From the North to the Middle Sea,
And he'd now sat down in the noble town
    Of the King of Saxony.

'October's deep dew its wet gossamer threw
    Upon Leipzig's lawns, leaf-strewn,
Where lately each fair avenue
    Wrought shade for summer noon.

'To westward two dull rivers crept
    Through miles of marsh and slough,
Whereover a streak of whiteness swept –
    The Bridge of Lindenau.

'Hard by, in the City, the One, care-tossed,
    Gloomed over his shrunken power;
And without the walls the hemming host
    Waxed denser every hour.

'He had speech that night on the morrow's designs
    With his chiefs by the bivouac fire,
While the belt of flames from the enemy's lines
    Flared nigher him yet and nigher.

'Three sky-lights then from the girdling trine
    Told, "Ready!" As they rose
Their flashes seemed his Judgment-Sign
    For bleeding Europe's woes.

"'Twas seen how the French watch-fires that night
    Glowed still and steadily;
And the Three rejoiced, for they read in the sight
    That the One disdained to flee…

' – Five hundred guns began the affray
    On next day morn at nine;
Such mad and mangling cannon-play
    Had never torn human line.

'Around the town three battles beat,
    Contracting like a gin;
As nearer marched the million feet
    Of columns closing in.

'The first battle nighed on the low Southern side;
    The second by the Western way;
The nearing of the third on the North was heard:
    – The French held all at bay.

'Against the first band did the Emperor stand;
    Against the second stood Ney;
Marmont[7] against the third gave the order-word:
    – Thus raged it throughout the day.

'Fifty thousand sturdy souls on those trampled plains
    and knolls,
    Who met the dawn hopefully,
And were lotted their shares in a quarrel not theirs,
    Dropt then in their agony.

'"O," the old folks said, "ye Preachers stern!
    O so-called Christian time!
When will men's swords to ploughshares turn?
    When come the promised prime?"...

' – The clash of horse and man which that day began,
    Closed not as evening wore;
And the morrow's armies, rear and van,
    Still mustered more and more.

'From the City towers the Confederate Powers
    Were eyed in glittering lines,
And up from the vast a murmuring passed
    As from a wood of pines.

'"'Tis well to cover a feeble skill
    By numbers!" scoffed He;
"But give me a third of their strength, I'd fill
    Half Hell with their soldiery!"

'All that day raged the war they waged,
    And again dumb night held reign,
Save that ever upspread from the dark deathbed
    A miles-wide pant of pain.

'Hard had striven brave Ney, the true Bertrand,
    Victor, and Augereau,
Bold Poniatowski, and Lauriston,[8]
    To stay their overthrow;

'But, as in the dream of one sick to death
    There comes a narrowing room
That pens him, body and limbs and breath,
    To wait a hideous doom,

'So to Napoleon, in the hush
    That held the town and towers
Through these dire nights, a creeping crush
    Seemed inborne with the hours.

'One road to the rearward, and but one,
    Did fitful Chance allow;
'Twas where the Pleiss' and Elster run –
    The Bridge of Lindenau.

'The nineteenth dawned. Down street and Platz
    The wasted French sank back,
Stretching long lines across the Flats
    And on the bridge-way track;

'When there surged on the sky an earthen wave,
    And stones, and men, as though
Some rebel churchyard crew updrave
    Their sepulchres from below.

'To Heaven is blown Bridge Lindenau;
    Wrecked regiments reel therefrom;

And rank and file in masses plough
    The sullen Elster-Strom.

'A gulf was Lindenau; and dead
    Were fifties, hundreds, tens;
And every current rippled red
    With Marshal's blood and men's.

'The smart Macdonald[9] swam therein,
    And barely won the verge;
Bold Poniatowski plunged him in
    Never to re-emerge.

'Then stayed the strife. The remnants wound
    Their Rhineward way pell-mell;
And thus did Leipzig City sound
    An Empire's passing bell;

'While in cavalcade, with band and blade,
    Came Marshals, Princes, Kings;
And the town was theirs... Ay, as simple maid,
    My mother saw these things!

'And whenever those notes in the street begin,
    I recall her, and that far scene,
And her acting of how the Allies marched in,
    And her touse of the tambourine!'

The Peasant's Confession

'Si le maréchal Grouchy avait été rejoint par l'officier que Napoléon lui avait expédié la veille à dix heures du soir, toute question eût disparu. Mais cet officier n'était point parvenu a sa destination, ainsi que le maréchal n'a cessé de l'affirmer toute sa vie, et il faut l'en croire, car autrement il n'aurait eu aucune raison pour hésiter. Cet officier avait-il été pris? avait-il passé a l'ennemi? C'est ce qu'on a toujours ignoré.'[10]
— THIERS: *Histoire de l'Empire*. 'Waterloo.'

Good Father!... 'Twas an eve in middle June,
    And war was waged anew
By great Napoleon, who for years had strewn
    Men's bones all Europe through.

Three nights ere this, with columned corps he'd crossed
    The Sambre at Charleroi,
To move on Brussels, where the English host
    Dallied in Parc and Bois.

The yestertide we'd heard the gloomy gun
    Growl through the long-sunned day
From Quatre-Bras and Ligny; till the dun
    Twilight suppressed the fray;

Albeit therein – as lated tongues bespoke –
    Brunswick's[11] high heart was drained,
And Prussia's Line and Landwehr, though unbroke,
    Stood cornered and constrained.

And at next noon-time Grouchy[12] slowly passed
    With thirty thousand men:
We hoped thenceforth no army, small or vast,
    Would trouble us again.

My hut lay deeply in a vale recessed,
    And never a soul seemed nigh
When, reassured at length, we went to rest –
    My children, wife, and I.

But what was this that broke our humble ease?
    What noise, above the rain,
Above the dripping of the poplar trees
    That smote along the pane?

– A call of mastery, bidding me arise,
    Compelled me to the door,
At which a horseman stood in martial guise –
    Splashed – sweating from every pore.

Had I seen Grouchy? Yes? Which track took he?
    Could I lead thither on? –
Fulfilment would ensure gold pieces three,
    Perchance more gifts anon.

'I bear the Emperor's mandate,' then he said,
    'Charging the Marshal straight
To strike between the double host ahead
    Ere they co-operate,

'Engaging Blücher[13] till the Emperor put
    Lord Wellington to flight,
And next the Prussians. This to set afoot
    Is my emprise to-night.'

I joined him in the mist; but, pausing, sought
    To estimate his say.

Grouchy had made for Wavre; and yet, on thought,
    I did not lead that way.

I mused: 'If Grouchy thus instructed be,
    The clash comes sheer hereon;
My farm is stript. While, as for pieces three,
    Money the French have none.

'Grouchy unwarned, moreo'er, the English win,
    And mine is left to me –
They buy, not borrow.' – Hence did I begin
    To lead him treacherously.

By Joidoigne, near to east, as we ondrew,
    Dawn pierced the humid air;
And eastward faced I with him, though I knew
    Never marched Grouchy there.

Near Ottignies we passed, across the Dyle
    (Lim'lette left far aside),
And thence direct toward Pervez and Noville
    Through green grain, till he cried:

'I doubt thy conduct, man! no track is here –
    I doubt thy gagèd word!'
Thereat he scowled on me, and pranced me near,
    And pricked me with his sword.

'Nay, Captain, hold! We skirt, not trace the course
    Of Grouchy,' said I then:
'As we go, yonder went he, with his force
    Of thirty thousand men.'

– At length noon nighed; when west, from Saint-John's-Mound,
    A hoarse artillery boomed,
And from Saint-Lambert's upland, chapel-crowned,
    The Prussian squadrons loomed.

Then to the wayless wet gray ground he leapt;
    'My mission fails!' he cried;
'Too late for Grouchy now to intercept,
    For, peasant, you have lied!'

He turned to pistol me. I sprang, and drew
    The sabre from his flank,
And 'twixt his nape and shoulder, ere he knew,
    I struck, and dead he sank.

I hid him deep in nodding rye and oat –
    His shroud green stalks and loam;
His requiem the corn-blade's husky note –
    And then I hastened home...

– Two armies writhe in coils of red and blue,
    And brass and iron clang
From Goumont, past the front of Waterloo,
    To Pap'lotte and Smohain.

The Guard Imperial wavered on the height;
    The Emperor's face grew glum;
'I sent,' he said, 'to Grouchy yesternight,
    And yet he does not come!'

'Twas then, Good Father, that the French espied,
    Streaking the summer land,

The men of Blücher. But the Emperor cried,
  'Grouchy is now at hand!'

And meanwhile Vand'leur, Vivian, Maitland, Kempt,[14]
  Met d'Erlon, Friant, Ney;[15]
But Grouchy – mis-sent, blamed, yet blame-exempt –
  Grouchy was far away.

By even, slain or struck, Michel the strong,
  Bold Travers, Dnop, Delord,
Smart Guyot, Reil-le, l'Heriter, Friant,
  Scattered that champaign o'er.

Fallen likewise wronged Duhesme, and skilled Lobau
  Did that red sunset see;
Colbert, Legros, Blancard!... And of the foe
  Picton and Ponsonby;

With Gordon, Canning, Blackman, Ompteda,
  L'Estrange, Delancey, Packe,
Grose, D'Oyly, Stables, Morice, Howard, Hay,
  Von Schwerin, Watzdorf, Boek,

Smith, Phelips, Fuller, Lind, and Battersby,
  And hosts of ranksmen round...
Memorials linger yet to speak to thee
  Of those that bit the ground![16]

The Guards' last column yielded; dykes of dead
  Lay between vale and ridge,
As, thinned yet closing, faint yet fierce, they sped
  In packs to Genappe Bridge.

Safe was my stock; my capple cow unslain;
    Intact each cock and hen;
But Grouchy far at Wavre all day had lain,
    And thirty thousand men.

O Saints, had I but lost my earing corn
    And saved the cause once prized!
O Saints, why such false witness had I borne
    When late I'd sympathised!...

So now, being old, my children eye askance
    My slowly dwindling store,
And crave my mite; till, worn with tarriance,
    I care for life no more.

To Almighty God henceforth I stand confessed,
    And Virgin-Saint Marie;
O Michael, John, and Holy Ones in rest,
    Entreat the Lord for me!

The Alarm

(1803)

See *The Trumpet-Major*
In memory of one of the writer's family who was a volunteer during the war
with Napoleon

In a ferny byway
    Near the great South-Wessex Highway,
  A homestead raised its breakfast-smoke aloft;
The dew-damps still lay steamless, for the sun had made no
        sky-way,
        And twilight cloaked the croft.

    'Twas hard to realise on
    This snug side the mute horizon
  That beyond it hostile armaments might steer,
Save from seeing in the porchway a fair woman weep with
        eyes on
        A harnessed Volunteer.

    In haste he'd flown there
    To his comely wife alone there,
  While marching south hard by, to still her fears,

For she soon would be a mother, and few messengers were
        known there
            In these campaigning years.

    'Twas time to be Good-bying,
    Since the assembly-hour was nighing
  In royal George's town at six that morn;
And betwixt its wharves and this retreat were ten good miles
        of hieing
            Ere ring of bugle-horn.

    'I've laid in food, Dear,
    And broached the spiced and brewed, Dear;
  And if our July hope should antedate,
Let the char-wench mount and gallop by the halterpath and
        wood, Dear,
            And fetch assistance straight.

    'As for Buonaparte, forget him;
    He's not like to land! But let him,
  Those strike with aim who strike for wives and sons!
And the war-boats built to float him; 'twere but wanted to
        upset him
            A slat from Nelson's guns!

    'But, to assure thee,
    And of creeping fears to cure thee,
  If he *should* be rumoured anchoring in the Road,
Drive with the nurse to Kingsbere; and let nothing thence
        allure thee
            Till we've him safe-bestowed.

'Now, to turn to marching matters: –
   I've my knapsack, firelock, spatters,
 Crossbelts, priming-horn, stock, bay'net, blackball, clay,
Pouch, magazine, flints, flint-box that at every quick-step
      clatters;
        …My heart, Dear; that must stay!'

   – With breathings broken
   Farewell was kissed unspoken,
 And they parted there as morning stroked the panes;
And the Volunteer went on, and turned, and twirled his glove
      for token,
        And took the coastward lanes.

   When above He'th Hills he found him,
   He saw, on gazing round him,
 The Barrow-Beacon burning – burning low,
As if, perhaps, uplighted ever since he'd homeward bound him;
        And it meant: Expect the Foe!

   Leaving the byway,
   And following swift the highway,
 Car and chariot met he, faring fast inland;
'He's anchored, Soldier!' shouted some: 'God save thee,
      marching thy way,
        Th'lt front him on the strand!'

   He slowed; he stopped; he paltered
   Awhile with self, and faltered,
 'Why courting misadventure shoreward roam?
To Molly, surely! Seek the woods with her till times have altered;
        Charity favours home.

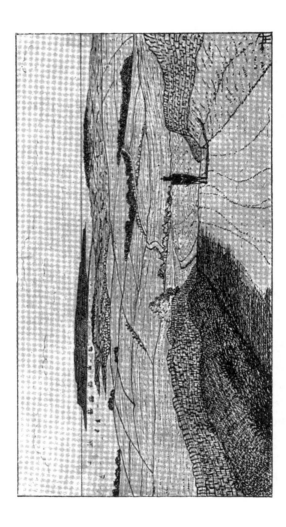

'Else, my denying
        He would come she'll read as lying –
    Think the Barrow-Beacon must have met my eyes –
That my words were not unwareness, but deceit of her,
        while trying
            My life to jeopardise.

    'At home is stocked provision,
        And to-night, without suspicion,
    We might bear it with us to a covert near;
Such sin, to save a childing wife, would earn it Christ's
        remission,
            Though none forgive it here!'

    While thus he, thinking,
        A little bird, quick drinking
    Among the crowfoot tufts the river bore,
Was tangled in their stringy arms, and fluttered, well-nigh
        sinking,
            Near him, upon the moor.

    He stepped in, reached, and seized it,
        And, preening, had released it
    But that a thought of Holy Writ occurred,
And Signs Divine ere battle, till it seemed him Heaven had
        pleased it
            As guide to send the bird.

    'O Lord, direct me!...
        Doth Duty now expect me
    To march a-coast, or guard my weak ones near?

Give this bird a flight according, that I thence know to
    elect me
        The southward or the rear.'

    He loosed his clasp; when, rising,
    The bird – as if surmising –
  Bore due to southward, crossing by the Froom,
And Durnover Great-Field and Fort, the soldier clear
    advising –
        Prompted he wist by Whom.

    Then on he panted
    By grim Mai-Don, and slanted
  Up the steep Ridge-way, hearkening betwixt whiles;
Till, nearing coast and harbour, he beheld the shore-line
    planted
        With Foot and Horse for miles.

    Mistrusting not the omen,
    He gained the beach, where Yeomen,
  Militia, Fencibles, and Pikemen bold,
With Regulars in thousands, were enmassed to meet
    the Foemen,
        Whose fleet had not yet shoaled.

    Captain and Colonel,
    Sere Generals, Ensigns vernal,
  Were there; of neighbour-natives, Michel, Smith,
Meggs, Bingham, Gambier, Cunningham, roused by the
    hued nocturnal
        Swoop on their land and kith.

But Buonaparte still tarried;
His project had miscarried;
At the last hour, equipped for victory,
The fleet had paused; his subtle combinations had been
parried
By British strategy.

Homeward returning
Anon, no beacons burning,
No alarms, the Volunteer, in modest bliss,
Te Deum sang with wife and friends: 'We praise Thee, Lord,
discerning
That Thou hast helped in this!'

Her Death and After

'Twas a death-bed summons, and forth I went
By the way of the Western Wall, so drear
On that winter night, and sought a gate –
      The home, by Fate,
   Of one I had long held dear.

And there, as I paused by her tenement,
And the trees shed on me their rime and hoar,
I thought of the man who had left her lone –
      Him who made her his own
   When I loved her, long before.

The rooms within had the piteous shine
That home-things wear when there's aught amiss;
From the stairway floated the rise and fall
      Of an infant's call,
   Whose birth had brought her to this.

Her life was the price she would pay for that whine –
For a child by the man she did not love.
'But let that rest for ever,' I said,
      And bent my tread
   To the chamber up above.

She took my hand in her thin white own,
And smiled her thanks – though nigh too weak –
And made them a sign to leave us there
      Then faltered, ere
   She could bring herself to speak.

''Twas to see you before I go – he'll condone
Such a natural thing now my time's not much –
When Death is so near it hustles hence
    All passioned sense
  Between woman and man as such!

'My husband is absent. As heretofore
The City detains him. But, in truth,
He has not been kind… I will speak no blame,
    But – the child is lame;
  O, I pray she may reach his ruth!

'Forgive past days – I can say no more –
Maybe if we'd wedded you'd now repine!…
But I treated you ill. I was punished. Farewell!
    – Truth shall I tell?
  Would the child were yours and mine!

'As a wife I was true. But, such my unease
That, could I insert a deed back in Time,
I'd make her yours, to secure your care;
    And the scandal bear,
  And the penalty for the crime!'

– When I had left, and the swinging trees
Rang above me, as lauding her candid say,
Another was I. Her words were enough:
    Came smooth, came rough,
  I felt I could live my day.

Next night she died; and her obsequies
In the Field of Tombs, by the Via renowned,

Had her husband's heed. His tendance spent,
 I often went
 And pondered by her mound.

All that year and the next year whiled,
And I still went thitherward in the gloom;
But the Town forgot her and her nook,
 And her husband took
 Another Love to his home.

And the rumour flew that the lame lone child
Whom she wished for its safety child of mine,
Was treated ill when offspring came
 Of the new-made dame,
 And marked a more vigorous line.

A smarter grief within me wrought
Than even at loss of her so dear;
Dead the being whose soul my soul suffused,
 Her child ill-used,
 I helpless to interfere!

One eve as I stood at my spot of thought
In the white-stoned Garth, brooding thus her wrong,
Her husband neared; and to shun his view
 By her hallowed mew
 I went from the tombs among

To the Cirque of the Gladiators which faced –
That haggard mark of Imperial Rome,
Whose Pagan echoes mock the chime

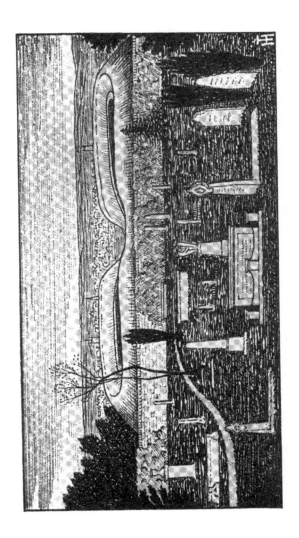

Of our Christian time:
It was void, and I inward clomb.

Scarce had night the sun's gold touch displaced
From the vast Rotund and the neighbouring dead
When her husband followed; bowed; half-passed,
    With lip upcast;
    Then, halting, sullenly said:

'It is noised that you visit my first wife's tomb.
Now, I gave her an honoured name to bear
While living, when dead. So I've claim to ask
    By what right you task
    My patience by vigiling there?

'There's decency even in death, I assume;
Preserve it, sir, and keep away;
For the mother of my first-born you
    Show mind undue!
    – Sir, I've nothing more to say.'

A desperate stroke discerned I then –
God pardon – or pardon not – the lie;
She had sighed that she wished (lest the child should pine
    Of slights) 'twere mine,
    So I said: 'But the father I.

'That you thought it yours is the way of men;
But I won her troth long ere your day:
You learnt how, in dying, she summoned me?
    'Twas in fealty.
    – Sir, I've nothing more to say,

'Save that, if you'll hand me my little maid,
I'll take her, and rear her, and spare you toil.
Think it more than a friendly act none can;
     I'm a lonely man,
   While you've a large pot to boil.

'If not, and you'll put it to ball or blade –
To-night, to-morrow night, anywhen –
I'll meet you here… But think of it,
     And in season fit
   Let me hear from you again.'

– Well, I went away, hoping; but nought I heard
Of my stroke for the child, till there greeted me
A little voice that one day came
     To my window-frame
   And babbled innocently:

'My father who's not my own, sends word
I'm to stay here, sir, where I belong!'
Next a writing came: 'Since the child was the fruit
     Of your lawless suit,
   Pray take her, to right a wrong.'

And I did. And I gave the child my love,
And the child loved me, and estranged us none.
But compunctions loomed; for I'd harmed the dead
     By what I'd said
   For the good of the living one.

– Yet though, God wot, I am sinner enough,
And unworthy the woman who drew me so,

Perhaps this wrong for her darling's good
    She forgives, or would,
  If only she could know!

The Dance at the Phoenix

To Jenny came a gentle youth
    From inland leazes lone,
His love was fresh as apple-blooth
    By Parrett, Yeo, or Tone.[17]
And duly he entreated her
To be his tender minister,
    And call him aye her own.

Fair Jenny's life had hardly been
    A life of modesty;
At Casterbridge experience keen
    Of many loves had she
From scarcely sixteen years above;
Among them sundry troopers of
    The King's-Own Cavalry.

But each with charger, sword, and gun,
    Had bluffed the Biscay wave;
And Jenny prized her gentle one

For all the love he gave.
She vowed to be, if they were wed,
His honest wife in heart and head
    From bride-ale hour to grave.

Wedded they were. Her husband's trust
    In Jenny knew no bound,
And Jenny kept her pure and just,
    Till even malice found
No sin or sign of ill to be
In one who walked so decently
    The duteous helpmate's round.

Two sons were born, and bloomed to men,
    And roamed, and were as not:
Alone was Jenny left again
    As ere her mind had sought
A solace in domestic joys,
And ere the vanished pair of boys
    Were sent to sun her cot.

She numbered near on sixty years,
    And passed as elderly,
When, in the street, with flush of fears,
    One day discovered she,
From shine of swords and thump of drum,
Her early loves from war had come,
    The King's-Own Cavalry.

She turned aside, and bowed her head
    Anigh Saint Peter's door;
'Alas for chastened thoughts!' she said;

'I'm faded now, and hoar,
And yet those notes – they thrill me through,
And those gay forms move me anew
  As in the years of yore!'...

'Twas Christmas, and the Phoenix Inn
  Was lit with tapers tall,
For thirty of the trooper men
  Had vowed to give a ball
As 'Theirs' had done ('twas handed down)
When lying in the selfsame town
  Ere Buonaparté's fall.

That night the throbbing 'Soldier's Joy',
  The measured tread and sway
Of 'Fancy-Lad' and 'Maiden Coy',
  Reached Jenny as she lay
Beside her spouse; till springtide blood
Seemed scouring through her like a flood
  That whisked the years away.

She rose, and rayed, and decked her head
  Where the bleached hairs ran thin;
Upon her cap two bows of red
  She fixed with hasty pin;
Unheard descending to the street,
She trod the flags with tune-led feet,
  And stood before the Inn.

Save for the dancers', not a sound
  Disturbed the icy air;
No watchman on his midnight round

Or traveller was there;
But over All-Saints', high and bright,
Pulsed to the music Sirius white,
     The Wain by Bullstake Square.

She knocked, but found her further stride
     Checked by a sergeant tall:
'Gay Granny, whence come you?' he cried;
     'This is a private ball.'
– 'No one has more right here than me!
Ere you were born, man,' answered she,
     'I knew the regiment all!'

'Take not the lady's visit ill!'
     Upspoke the steward free;
'We lack sufficient partners still,
     So, prithee let her be!'
They seized and whirled her 'mid the maze,
And Jenny felt as in the days
     Of her immodesty.

Hour chased each hour, and night advanced;
     She sped as shod with wings;
Each time and every time she danced –
     Reels, jigs, poussettes, and flings:
They cheered her as she soared and swooped,
(She'd learnt ere art in dancing drooped
     From hops to slothful swings).

The favourite Quick-step 'Speed the Plough' –
     (Cross hands, cast off, and wheel) –
'The Triumph', 'Sylph', 'The Row-dow-dow',

Famed 'Major Malley's Reel',
'The Duke of York's', 'The Fairy Dance',
'The Bridge of Lodi' (brought from France),
    She beat out, toe and heel.

The 'Fall of Paris' clanged its close,
    And Peter's chime told four,
When Jenny, bosom-beating, rose
    To seek her silent door.
They tiptoed in escorting her,
Lest stroke of heel or clink of spur
    Should break her goodman's snore.

The fire that late had burnt fell slack
    When lone at last stood she;
Her nine-and-fifty years came back;
    She sank upon her knee
Beside the durn, and like a dart
A something arrowed through her heart
    In shoots of agony.

Their footsteps died as she leant there,
    Lit by the morning star
Hanging above the moorland, where
    The aged elm-rows are;
And, as o'ernight, from Pummery Ridge
To Maembury Ring and Standfast Bridge
    No life stirred, near or far.

Though inner mischief worked amain,
    She reached her husband's side;
Where, toil-weary, as he had lain

Beneath the patchwork pied
When yestereve she'd forthward crept,
And as unwitting, still he slept
   Who did in her confide.

A tear sprang as she turned and viewed
   His features free from guile;
She kissed him long, as when, just wooed,
   She chose his domicile.
She felt she could have given her life
To be the single-hearted wife
   That she had been erstwhile.

Time wore to six. Her husband rose
   And struck the steel and stone;
He glanced at Jenny, whose repose
   Seemed deeper than his own.
With dumb dismay, on closer sight,
He gathered sense that in the night,
   Or morn, her soul had flown.

When told that some too mighty strain
   For one so many-yeared
Had burst her bosom's master-vein,
   His doubts remained unstirred.
His Jenny had not left his side
Betwixt the eve and morning-tide:
   – The King's said not a word.

Well! times are not as times were then,
   Nor fair ones half so free;
And truly they were martial men,

The King's-Own Cavalry.
And when they went from Casterbridge
And vanished over Mellstock Ridge,
    'Twas saddest morn to see.

The Casterbridge Captains
(Khyber Pass, 1842)

A tradition of J.B.L—, T.G.B—, and J.L—.

Three captains went to Indian wars,
    And only one returned:
Their mate of yore, he singly wore
    The laurels all had earned.

At home he sought the ancient aisle
    Wherein, untrumped of fame,
The three had sat in pupilage,
    And each had carved his name.

The names, rough-hewn, of equal size,
    Stood on the panel still;
Unequal since. – ''Twas theirs to aim,
    Mine was it to fulfil!'

– 'Who saves his life shall lose it, friends!'
    Outspake the preacher then,
Unweeting he his listener, who
    Looked at the names again.

That he had come and they'd been stayed,
    'Twas but the chance of war:
Another chance, and they'd sat here,
    And he had lain afar.

Yet saw he something in the lives
   Of those who'd ceased to live
That sphered them with a majesty
   Which living failed to give.

Transcendent triumph in return
   No longer lit his brain;
Transcendence rayed the distant urn
   Where slept the fallen twain.

A Sign-Seeker

I mark the months in liveries dank and dry,
  The noontides many-shaped and hued;
  I see the nightfall shades subtrude,
And hear the monotonous hours clang negligently by.

I view the evening bonfires of the sun
  On hills where morning rains have hissed;
  The eyeless countenance of the mist
Pallidly rising when the summer droughts are done.

I have seen the lightning-blade, the leaping star,
  The cauldrons of the sea in storm,
  Have felt the earthquake's lifting arm,
And trodden where abysmal fires and snow-cones are.

I learn to prophesy the hid eclipse,
  The coming of eccentric orbs;
  To mete the dust the sky absorbs,
To weigh the sun, and fix the hour each planet dips.

I witness fellow earth-men surge and strive;
  Assemblies meet, and throb, and part;
  Death's soothing finger, sorrow's smart;
– All the vast various moils that mean a world alive.

But that I fain would wot of shuns my sense –
    Those sights of which old prophets tell,
    Those signs the general word so well,
Vouchsafed to their unheed, denied my long suspense.

In graveyard green, behind his monument
    To glimpse a phantom parent, friend,
    Wearing his smile, and 'Not the end!'
Outbreathing softly: that were blest enlightenment;

Or, if a dead Love's lips, whom dreams reveal
    When midnight imps of King Decay
    Delve sly to solve me back to clay,
Should leave some print to prove her spirit-kisses real;

Or, when Earth's Frail lie bleeding of her Strong,
    If some Recorder, as in Writ,
    Near to the weary scene should flit
And drop one plume as pledge that Heaven inscrolls the
    wrong.

– There are who, rapt to heights of trancéd trust,
    These tokens claim to feel and see,
    Read radiant hints of times to be –
Of heart to heart returning after dust to dust.

Such scope is granted not to lives like mine…
    I have lain in dead men's beds, have walked
    The tombs of those with whom I'd talked,
Called many a gone and goodly one to shape a sign,

And panted for response. But none replies;
   No warnings loom, nor whisperings
   To open out my limitings,
And Nescience mutely muses: When a man falls he lies.

My Cicely
(17–)

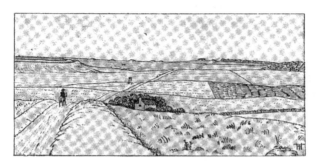

'Alive?' – And I leapt in my wonder,
    Was faint of my joyance,
And grasses and grove shone in garments
    Of glory to me.

'She lives, in a plenteous well-being,
    To-day as aforehand;
The dead bore the name – though a rare one –
    The name that bore she.'

She lived... I, afar in the city
    Of frenzy-led factions,
Had squandered green years and maturer
    In bowing the knee

To Baals illusive and specious,
    Till chance had there voiced me
That one I loved vainly in nonage
    Had ceased her to be.

The passion the planets had scowled on,
    And change had let dwindle,
Her death-rumour smartly relifted
    To full apogee.

I mounted a steed in the dawning
    With acheful remembrance,
And made for the ancient West Highway
    To far Exonb'ry.

Passing heaths, and the House of Long Sieging,
    I neared the thin steeple
That tops the fair fane of Poore's olden
    Episcopal see;

And, changing anew my onbearer,
    I traversed the downland
Whereon the bleak hill-graves of Chieftains
    Bulge barren of tree;

And still sadly onward I followed
    That Highway the Icen,
Which trails its pale riband down Wessex
    O'er lynchet and lea.

Along through the Stour-bordered Forum,
    Where Legions had wayfared,
And where the slow river upglasses
    Its green canopy,

And by Weatherbury Castle, and thencefrom
    Through Casterbridge held I

Still on, to entomb her my vision
  Saw stretched pallidly.

No highwayman's trot blew the night-wind
  To me so life-weary,
But only the creak of the gibbets
  Or waggoners' jee.

Triple-ramparted Maidon gloomed grayly
  Above me from southward,
And north the hill-fortress of Eggar,
  And square Pummerie.

The Nine-Pillared Cromlech, the Bride-streams,
  The Axe, and the Otter
I passed, to the gate of the city
  Where Exe scents the sea;

Till, spent, in the graveacre pausing,
  I learnt 'twas not my Love
To whom Mother Church had just murmured
  A last lullaby.

– 'Then, where dwells the Canon's kinswoman,
  My friend of aforetime?' –
('Twas hard to repress my heart-heavings
  And new ecstasy.)

'She wedded.' – 'Ah!' – 'Wedded beneath her –
  She keeps the stage-hostel
Ten miles hence, beside the great Highway –
  The famed Lions-Three.

'Her spouse was her lackey – no option
 'Twixt wedlock and worse things;
A lapse over-sad for a lady
 Of her pedigree!'

I shuddered, said nothing, and wandered
 To shades of green laurel:
Too ghastly had grown those first tidings
 So brightsome of blee!

For, on my ride hither, I'd halted
 Awhile at the Lions,
And her – her whose name had once opened
 My heart as a key –

I'd looked on, unknowing, and witnessed
 Her jests with the tapsters,
Her liquor-fired face, her thick accents
 In naming her fee.

'O God, why this seeming derision!'
 I cried in my anguish:
'O once Loved, O fair Unforgotten –
 That Thing – meant it thee!

'Inurned and at peace, lost but sainted,
 Were grief I could compass;
Depraved – 'tis for Christ's poor dependent
 A cruel decree!'

I backed on the Highway; but passed not
 The hostel. Within there

Too mocking to Love's re-expression
　　Was Time's repartee!

Uptracking where Legions had wayfared,
　　By cromlechs unstoried,
And lynchets, and sepultured Chieftains,
　　In self-colloquy,

A feeling stirred in me and strengthened
　　That *she* was not my Love,
But she of the garth, who lay rapt in
　　Her long reverie.

And thence till to-day I persuade me
　　That this was the true one;
That Death stole intact her young dearness
　　And innocency.

Frail-witted, illuded they call me;
　　I may be. 'Tis better
To dream than to own the debasement
　　Of sweet Cicely.

Moreover I rate it unseemly
　　To hold that kind Heaven
Could work such device – to her ruin
　　And my misery.

So, lest I disturb my choice vision,
　　I shun the West Highway,
Even now, when the knaps ring with rhythms
　　From blackbird and bee;

And feel that with slumber half-conscious
   She rests in the church-hay,
Her spirit unsoiled as in youth-time
   When lovers were we.

Her Immortality

Upon a noon I pilgrimed through
   A pasture, mile by mile,
Unto the place where I last saw
   My dead Love's living smile.

And sorrowing I lay me down
   Upon the heated sod:
It seemed as if my body pressed
   The very ground she trod.

I lay, and thought; and in a trance
   She came and stood me by –
The same, even to the marvellous ray
   That used to light her eye.

'You draw me, and I come to you,
   My faithful one,' she said,
In voice that had the moving tone
   It bore ere breath had fled.

She said: ''Tis seven years since I died:
   Few now remember me;
My husband clasps another bride;
   My children's love has she.

'My brethren, sisters, and my friends
   Care not to meet my sprite:
Who prized me most I did not know
   Till I passed down from sight.'

I said: 'My days are lonely here;
        I need thy smile alway:
I'll use this night my ball or blade,
        And join thee ere the day.'

A tremor stirred her tender lips,
        Which parted to dissuade:
'That cannot be, O friend,' she cried;
        'Think, I am but a Shade!

'A Shade but in its mindful ones
        Has immortality;
By living, me you keep alive,
        By dying you slay me.

'In you resides my single power
        Of sweet continuance here;
On your fidelity I count
        Through many a coming year.'

– I started through me at her plight,
        So suddenly confessed:
Dismissing late distaste for life,
        I craved its bleak unrest.

'I will not die, my One of all! –
        To lengthen out thy days
I'll guard me from minutest harms
        That may invest my ways!'

She smiled and went. Since then she comes
        Oft when her birth-moon climbs,

Or at the seasons' ingresses
    Or anniversary times;

But grows my grief. When I surcease,
    Through whom alone lives she,
Ceases my Love, her words, her ways,
    Never again to be!

The Ivy-Wife

I longed to love a full-boughed beech
    And be as high as he:
I stretched an arm within his reach,
    And signalled unity.
But with his drip he forced a breach,
    And tried to poison me.

I gave the grasp of partnership
    To one of other race –
A plane: he barked him strip by strip
    From upper bough to base;
And me therewith; for gone my grip,
    My arms could not enlace.

In new affection next I strove
    To coll an ash I saw,
And he in trust received my love;
    Till with my soft green claw
I cramped and bound him as I wove…
    Such was my love: ha-ha!

By this I gained his strength and height
    Without his rivalry.
But in my triumph I lost sight
    Of afterhaps. Soon he,
Being bark-bound, flagged, snapped, fell outright,
    And in his fall felled me!

A Meeting with Despair

As evening shaped I found me on a moor
    Which sight could scarce sustain:
The black lean land, of featureless contour,
    Was like a tract in pain.

'This scene, like my own life,' I said, 'is one
    Where many glooms abide;
Toned by its fortune to a deadly dun –
    Lightless on every side.

I glanced aloft and halted, pleasure-caught
    To see the contrast there:
The ray-lit clouds gleamed glory; and I thought,
    'There's solace everywhere!'

Then bitter self-reproaches as I stood
    I dealt me silently
As one perverse – misrepresenting Good
    In graceless mutiny.

Against the horizon's dim-discernèd wheel
    A form rose, strange of mould:
That he was hideous, hopeless, I could feel
    Rather than could behold.

''Tis a dead spot, where even the light lies spent
    To darkness!' croaked the Thing.
'Not if you look aloft!' said I, intent
    On my new reasoning.

'Yea – but await awhile!' he cried. 'Ho-ho! –
   Look now aloft and see!'
I looked. There, too, sat night: Heaven's radiant show
   Had gone. Then chuckled he.

Unknowing

When, soul in soul reflected,
We breathed an aethered air,
　　When we neglected
　　All things elsewhere,
And left the friendly friendless
To keep our love aglow,
　　We deemed it endless...
　　– We did not know!

When, by mad passion goaded,
We planned to hie away,
　　But, unforeboded,
　　The storm-shafts gray
So heavily down-pattered
That none could forthward go,
　　Our lives seemed shattered...
　　– We did not know!

When I found you, helpless lying,
And you waived my deep misprise,
　　And swore me, dying,
　　In phantom-guise
To wing to me when grieving,
And touch away my woe,
　　We kissed, believing...
　　– We did not know!

But though, your powers outreckoning,
You hold you dead and dumb,
　　Or scorn my beckoning,

And will not come;
And I say, "'Twere mood ungainly
To store her memory so:'
    I say it vainly –
    I feel and know!

Friends Beyond

William Dewy, Tranter Reuben, Farmer Ledlow late
    at plough,
  Robert's kin, and John's, and Ned's,
And the Squire, and Lady Susan, lie in Mellstock
    churchyard now!

'Gone,' I call them, gone for good, that group of local
    hearts and heads;
  Yet at mothy curfew-tide,
And at midnight when the noon-heat breathes it back
    from walls and leads,

They've a way of whispering to me – fellow-wight
    who yet abide –
  In the muted, measured note
Of a ripple under archways, or a lone cave's
    stillicide:

'We have triumphed: this achievement turns the bane
    to antidote,
  Unsuccesses to success,
– Many thought-worn eves and morrows to a morrow
    free of thought.

'No more need we corn and clothing, feel of old
    terrestrial stress;
  Chill detraction stirs no sigh;
Fear of death has even bygone us: death gave all that
    we possess.'

W.D.—'Ye mid burn the wold bass-viol that I set such
      vallie by.'

Squire—'You may hold the manse in fee,
      You may wed my spouse, my children's memory
      of me may decry.'

Lady— 'You may have my rich brocades, my laces; take each
      household key;
      Ransack coffer, desk, bureau;
    Quiz the few poor treasures hid there, con the letters
      kept by me.'

Far.— 'Ye mid zell my favourite heifer, ye mid let the
      charlock grow,
      Foul the grinterns, give up thrift.'

Wife— 'If ye break my best blue china, children, I shan't care
      or ho.'

All— 'We've no wish to hear the tidings, how the people's
      fortunes shift;
      What your daily doings are;
    Who are wedded, born, divided; if your lives beat
      slow or swift.

    'Curious not the least are we if our intents you make
      or mar,
      If you quire to our old tune,
    If the City stage still passes, if the weirs still roar afar.'

    – Thus, with very gods' composure, freed those
      crosses late and soon
      Which, in life, the Trine allow

(Why, none witteth), and ignoring all that haps
    beneath the moon,

William Dewy, Tranter Reuben, Farmer Ledlow late
    at plough,
  Robert's kin, and John's, and Ned's,
And the Squire, and Lady Susan, murmur mildly to
    me now.

To Outer Nature

Show thee as I thought thee
When I early sought thee,
   Omen-scouting,
   All undoubting
Love alone had wrought thee –

Wrought thee for my pleasure,
Planned thee as a measure
   For expounding
   And resounding
Glad things that men treasure.

O for but a moment
Of that old endowment –
   Light to gaily
   See thy daily
Irisèd embowment!

But such re-adorning
Time forbids with scorning –
   Makes me see things
   Cease to be things
They were in my morning.

Fad'st thou, glow-forsaken,
Darkness-overtaken!
   Thy first sweetness,
   Radiance, meetness,
None shall re-awaken.

Why not sempiternal
Thou and I? Our vernal
    Brightness keeping,
    Time outleaping;
Passed the hodiernal!

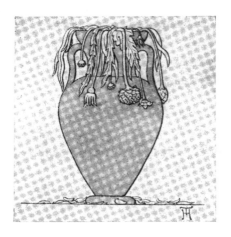

Thoughts of Phena
At News of her Death

    Not a line of her writing have I,
        Not a thread of her hair,
No mark of her late time as dame in her dwelling, whereby
        I may picture her there;
    And in vain do I urge my unsight
        To conceive my lost prize
At her close, whom I knew when her dreams were
    upbrimming with light,
        And with laughter her eyes.

    What scenes spread around her last days,
        Sad, shining, or dim?
Did her gifts and compassions enray and enarch her sweet ways
        With an aureate nimb?
    Or did life-light decline from her years,
        And mischances control
Her full day-star; unease, or regret, or forebodings, or fears
        Disennoble her soul?

    Thus I do but the phantom retain
        Of the maiden of yore
As my relic; yet haply the best of her – fined in my brain
        It maybe the more
    That no line of her writing have I,
        Nor a thread of her hair,
No mark of her late time as dame in her dwelling, whereby
        I may picture her there.

March 1890

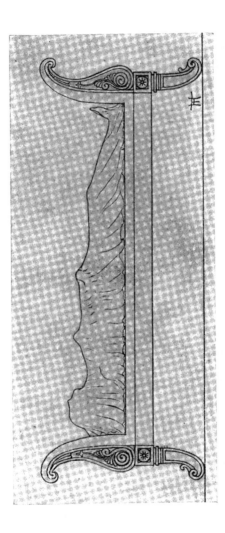

Middle-Age Enthusiasms
To M.H.

We passed where flag and flower
Signalled a jocund throng;
We said: 'Go to, the hour
Is apt!' – and joined the song;
And, kindling, laughed at life and care,
Although we knew no laugh lay there.

We walked where shy birds stood
Watching us, wonder-dumb;
Their friendship met our mood;
We cried: 'We'll often come:
We'll come morn, noon, eve, everywhen!'
– We doubted we should come again.

We joyed to see strange sheens
Leap from quaint leaves in shade;
A secret light of greens
They'd for their pleasure made.
We said: 'We'll set such sorts as these!'
– We knew with night the wish would cease.

'So sweet the place,' we said,
'Its tacit tales so dear,
Our thoughts, when breath has sped,
Will meet and mingle here!'...
'Words!' mused we. 'Passed the mortal door,
Our thoughts will reach this nook no more.'

In a Wood

See *The Woodlanders*[18]

Pale beech and pine-tree blue,
  Set in one clay,
Bough to bough cannot you
  Bide out your day?
When the rains skim and skip,
Why mar sweet comradeship,
Blighting with poison-drip
  Neighbourly spray?

Heart-halt and spirit-lame,
  City-opprest,
Unto this wood I came
  As to a nest;
Dreaming that sylvan peace
Offered the harrowed ease –
Nature a soft release
  From men's unrest.

But, having entered in,
  Great growths and small
Show them to men akin –
  Combatants all!
Sycamore shoulders oak,
Bines the slim sapling yoke,
Ivy-spun halters choke
  Elms stout and tall.

Touches from ash, O wych,
   Sting you like scorn!
You, too, brave hollies, twitch
   Sidelong from thorn.
Even the rank poplars bear
Illy a rival's air,
Cankering in black despair
   If overborne.

Since, then, no grace I find
   Taught me of trees,
Turn I back to my kind,
   Worthy as these.
There at least smiles abound,
There discourse trills around,
There, now and then, are found
   Life-loyalties.

1887: 1896

To a Lady
Offended by a Book of the Writer's

Now that my page upcloses, doomed, maybe,
Never to press thy cosy cushions more,
Or wake thy ready Yeas as heretofore,
Or stir thy gentle vows of faith in me:

Knowing thy natural receptivity,
I figure that, as flambeaux banish eve,
My sombre image, warped by insidious heave
Of those less forthright, must lose place in thee.

So be it. I have borne such. Let thy dreams
Of me and mine diminish day by day,
And yield their space to shine of smugger things;
Till I shape to thee but in fitful gleams,
And then in far and feeble visitings,
And then surcease. Truth will be truth alway.

To an Orphan Child
A Whimsey

Ah, child, thou art but half thy darling mother's;
    Hers couldst thou wholly be,
My light in thee would outglow all in others;
    She would relive to me.
But niggard Nature's trick of birth
    Bars, lest she overjoy,
Renewal of the loved on earth
    Save with alloy.

The Dame has no regard, alas, my maiden,
    For love and loss like mine –
No sympathy with mind-sight memory-laden;
    Only with fickle eyne.
To her mechanic artistry
    My dreams are all unknown,
And why I wish that thou couldst be
    But One's alone!

Nature's Questioning

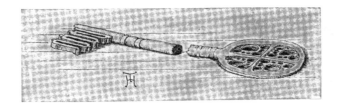

When I look forth at dawning, pool,
　　Field, flock, and lonely tree,
　　All seem to gaze at me
Like chastened children sitting silent in a school;

　　Their faces dulled, constrained, and worn,
　　　As though the master's ways
　　　Through the long teaching days
Their first terrestrial zest had chilled and overborne.

　　And on them stirs, in lippings mere
　　　(As if once clear in call,
　　　But now scarce breathed at all) –
'We wonder, ever wonder, why we find us here!

　　'Has some Vast Imbecility,
　　　Mighty to build and blend,
　　　But impotent to tend,
Framed us in jest, and left us now to hazardry?

　　'Or come we of an Automaton
　　　Unconscious of our pains?…

Or are we live remains
Of Godhead dying downwards, brain and eye now gone?

'Or is it that some high Plan betides,
As yet not understood,
Of Evil stormed by Good,
We the Forlorn Hope over which Achievement strides?'

Thus things around. No answerer I…
Meanwhile the winds, and rains,
And Earth's old glooms and pains
Are still the same, and gladdest Life Death neighbours nigh.

The Impercipient
(at a Cathedral Service)

That from this bright believing band
    An outcast I should be,
That faiths by which my comrades stand
    Seem fantasies to me,
And mirage-mists their Shining Land,
    Is a drear destiny.

Why thus my soul should be consigned
    To infelicity,
Why always I must feel as blind
    To sights my brethren see,
Why joys they've found I cannot find,
    Abides a mystery.

Since heart of mine knows not that ease
    Which they know; since it be
That He who breathes All's Well to these
    Breathes no All's-Well to me,
My lack might move their sympathies
    And Christian charity!

I am like a gazer who should mark
    An inland company
Standing upfingered, with, 'Hark! hark!
    The glorious distant sea!'
And feel, 'Alas, 'tis but yon dark
    And wind-swept pine to me!'

Yet I would bear my shortcomings
    With meet tranquillity,
But for the charge that blessed things
    I'd liefer have unbe.
O, doth a bird deprived of wings
    Go earth-bound wilfully!

                    * * *

Enough. As yet disquiet clings
    About us. Rest shall we.

At an Inn

When we as strangers sought
   Their catering care,
Veiled smiles bespoke their thought
   Of what we were.
They warmed as they opined
   Us more than friends –
That we had all resigned
   For love's dear ends.

And that swift sympathy
   With living love
Which quicks the world – maybe
   The spheres above,
Made them our ministers,
   Moved them to say,
'Ah, God, that bliss like theirs
   Would flush our day!'

And we were left alone
   As Love's own pair;
Yet never the love-light shone
   Between us there!
But that which chilled the breath
   Of afternoon,
And palsied unto death
   The pane-fly's tune.

The kiss their zeal foretold,
   And now deemed come,
Came not: within his hold

Love lingered numb.
Why cast he on our port
  A bloom not ours?
Why shaped us for his sport
  In after-hours?

As we seemed we were not
  That day afar,
And now we seem not what
  We aching are.
O severing sea and land,
  O laws of men,
Ere death, once let us stand
  As we stood then!

The Slow Nature
(An Incident of Froom Valley)

'Thy husband – poor, poor Heart! – is dead –
    Dead, out by Moreford Rise;
A bull escaped the barton-shed,
    Gored him, and there he lies!'

– 'Ha, ha – go away! 'Tis a tale, methink,
    Thou joker Kit!' laughed she.
'I've known thee many a year, Kit Twink,
    And ever hast thou fooled me!'

– 'But, Mistress Damon – I can swear
    Thy goodman John is dead!
And soon th'lt hear their feet who bear
    His body to his bed.'

So unwontedly sad was the merry man's face –
    That face which had long deceived –
That she gazed and gazed; and then could trace
    The truth there; and she believed.

She laid a hand on the dresser-ledge,
    And scanned far Egdon-side;
And stood; and you heard the wind-swept sedge
    And the rippling Froom; till she cried:

'O my chamber's untidied, unmade my bed
    Though the day has begun to wear!
'What a slovenly hussif!' it will be said,
    When they all go up my stair!'

She disappeared; and the joker stood
  Depressed by his neighbour's doom,
And amazed that a wife struck to widowhood
  Thought first of her unkempt room.

But a fortnight thence she could take no food,
  And she pined in a slow decay;
While Kit soon lost his mournful mood
  And laughed in his ancient way.

1894

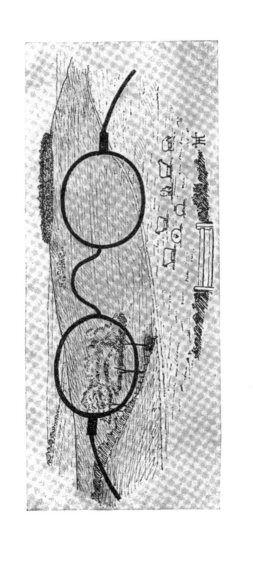

In a Eweleaze Near Weatherbury

The years have gathered grayly
　　Since I danced upon this leaze
With one who kindled gaily
　　Love's fitful ecstasies!
But despite the term as teacher,
　　I remain what I was then
In each essential feature
　　Of the fantasies of men.

Yet I note the little chisel
　　Of never-napping Time,
Defacing ghast and grizzel
　　The blazon of my prime.
When at night he thinks me sleeping,
　　I feel him boring sly
Within my bones, and heaping
　　Quaintest pains for by-and-by.

Still, I'd go the world with Beauty,
　　I would laugh with her and sing,
I would shun divinest duty
　　To resume her worshipping.
But she'd scorn my brave endeavour,
　　She would not balm the breeze
By murmuring 'Thine for ever!'
　　As she did upon this leaze.

1890

The Fire at Tranter Sweatley's

They had long met o' Zundays – her true love and she –
    And at junketings, maypoles, and flings;
But she bode wi' a thirtover uncle, and he
Swore by noon and by night that her goodman should be
Naibour Sweatley – a gaffer oft weak at the knee
From taking o' sommat more cheerful than tea –
    Who tranted, and moved people's things.

She cried, 'O pray pity me!' Nought would he hear;
    Then with wild rainy eyes she obeyed.
She chid when her Love was for clinking off wi' her.
The pa'son was told, as the season drew near
To throw over pu'pit the names of the peäir
    As fitting one flesh to be made.

The wedding-day dawned and the morning drew on;
    The couple stood bridegroom and bride;
The evening was passed, and when midnight had gone
The folks horned out, 'God save the King,' and anon
    The two home-along gloomily hied.

The lover Tim Tankens mourned heart-sick and drear
    To be thus of his darling deprived:
He roamed in the dark ath'art field, mound, and mere,
And, a'most without knowing it, found himself near
The house of the tranter, and now of his Dear,
    Where the lantern-light showed 'em arrived.

The bride sought her cham'er so calm and so pale
    That a Northern had thought her resigned;

But to eyes that had seen her in tide-times of weal,
Like the white cloud o' smoke, the red battle-field's vail,
   That look spak' of havoc behind.

The bridegroom yet laitered a beaker to drain,
   Then reeled to the linhay for more,
When the candle-snoff kindled some chaff from his grain –
Flames spread, and red vlankers, wi' might and wi' main,
   And round beams, thatch, and chimley-tun roar.

Young Tim away yond, rafted up by the light,
   Through brimble and underwood tears,
Till he comes to the orchet, when crooping thereright
In the lewth of a codlin-tree, bivering wi' fright,
Wi' on'y her night-rail to screen her from sight,
   His lonesome young Barbree appears.

Her cwold little figure half-naked he views
   Played about by the frolicsome breeze,
Her light-tripping totties, her ten little tooes,
All bare and besprinkled wi' Fall's chilly dews,
While her great gallied eyes, through her hair hanging loose,
   Sheened as stars through a tardle o' trees.

She eyed en; and, as when a weir-hatch is drawn,
   Her tears, penned by terror afore,
With a rushing of sobs in a shower were strawn,
Till her power to pour 'em seemed wasted and gone
   From the heft o' misfortune she bore.

'O Tim, my *own* Tim I must call 'ee – I will!
   All the world ha' turned round on me so!

Can you help her who loved 'ee, though acting so ill?
Can you pity her misery – feel for her still?
When worse than her body so quivering and chill
   Is her heart in its winter o' woe!

'I think I mid almost ha' borne it,' she said,
   'Had my griefs one by one come to hand;
But O, to be slave to thik husbird for bread,
And then, upon top o' that, driven to wed,
And then, upon top o' that, burnt out o' bed,
   Is more than my nater can stand!'

Tim's soul like a lion 'ithin en outsprung –
(Tim had a great soul when his feelings were wrung) –
   'Feel for 'ee, dear Barbree?' he cried;
And his warm working-jacket about her he flung,
Made a back, horsed her up, till behind him she clung
Like a chiel on a gipsy, her figure uphung
   By the sleeves that around her he tied.

Over piggeries, and mixens, and apples, and hay,
   They lumpered straight into the night;
And finding bylong where a halter-path lay,
At dawn reached Tim's house, on'y seen on their way
By a naibour or two who were up wi' the day;
   But they gathered no clue to the sight.

Then tender Tim Tankens he searched here and there
   For some garment to clothe her fair skin;
But though he had breeches and waistcoats to spare,
He had nothing quite seemly for Barbree to wear,

Who, half shrammed to death, stood and cried on a chair
　　At the caddle she found herself in.

There was one thing to do, and that one thing he did,
　　He lent her some clouts of his own,
And she took 'em perforce; and while in 'em she slid,
Tim turned to the winder, as modesty bid,
Thinking, 'O that the picter my duty keeps hid
　　To the sight o' my eyes mid be shown!'

In the tallet he stowed her; there huddied she lay,
　　Shortening sleeves, legs, and tails to her limbs;
But most o' the time in a mortal bad way,
Well knowing that there'd be the divel to pay
If 'twere found that, instead o' the elements' prey,
　　She was living in lodgings at Tim's.

'Where's the tranter?' said men and boys;
　　　'where can er be?'
　　'Where's the tranter?' said Barbree alone.
'Where on e'th is the tranter?' said everybod-y:
They sifted the dust of his perished roof-tree,
　　And all they could find was a bone.

Then the uncle cried, 'Lord, pray have mercy on me!'
　　And in terror began to repent.
But before 'twas complete, and till sure she was free,
Barbree drew up her loft-ladder, tight turned her key –
Tim bringing up breakfast and dinner and tea –
　　Till the news of her hiding got vent.

Then followed the custom-kept rout, shout, and flare
Of a skimmington-ride through the naibourhood, ere
    Folk had proof o' wold Sweatley's decay.
Whereupon decent people all stood in a stare,
Saying Tim and his lodger should risk it, and pair:
So he took her to church. An' some laughing lads there
Cried to Tim, 'After Sweatley!' She said, 'I declare
    I stand as a maiden to-day!'

Written 1866; printed 1875

Heiress and Architect

For A.W.B.

She sought the Studios, beckoning to her side
An arch-designer, for she planned to build.
He was of wise contrivance, deeply skilled
In every intervolve of high and wide –
    Well fit to be her guide.

    'Whatever it be,'
    Responded he,
With cold, clear voice, and cold, clear view,
'In true accord with prudent fashionings
For such vicissitudes as living brings,
And thwarting not the law of stable things,
    That will I do.'

'Shape me,' she said, 'high halls with tracery
And open ogive-work, that scent and hue
Of buds, and travelling bees, may come in
    through,
The note of birds, and singings of the sea,
    For these are much to me.'

    'An idle whim!'
    Broke forth from him
Whom nought could warm to gallantries:
'Cede all these buds and birds, the zephyr's call,
And scents, and hues, and things that falter all,
And choose as best the close and surly wall,
    For winters freeze.'

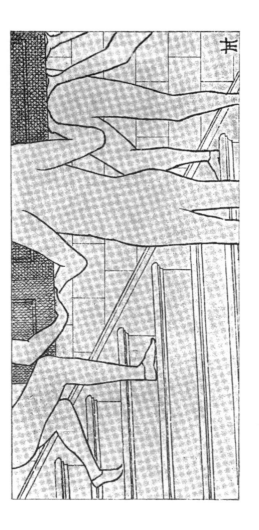

'Then frame,' she cried, 'wide fronts of crystal glass,
That I may show my laughter and my light –
Light like the sun's by day, the stars' by night –
Till rival heart-queens, envying, wail, "Alas,
    Her glory!" as they pass.'

        'O maid misled!'
        He sternly said,
Whose facile foresight pierced her dire;
'Where shall abide the soul when, sick of glee,
It shrinks, and hides, and prays no eye may see?
Those house them best who house for secrecy,
        For you will tire.'

'A little chamber, then, with swan and dove
Ranged thickly, and engrailed with rare device
Of reds and purples, for a Paradise
Wherein my Love may greet me, I my Love,
    When he shall know thereof?'

        'This, too, is ill,'
        He answered still,
The man who swayed her like a shade.
'An hour will come when sight of such sweet nook
Would bring a bitterness too sharp to brook,
When brighter eyes have won away his look;
        For you will fade.'

Then said she faintly: 'O, contrive some way –
Some narrow winding turret, quite mine own,
To reach a loft where I may grieve alone!

It is a slight thing; hence do not, I pray,
   This last dear fancy slay!'

    'Such winding ways
    Fit not your days,'
Said he, the man of measuring eye;
'I must even fashion as my rule declares,
To wit: Give space (since life ends unawares)
To hale a coffined corpse adown the stairs;
    For you will die.'

1867

The Two Men

There were two youths of equal age,
Wit, station, strength, and parentage;
They studied at the selfsame schools,
And shaped their thoughts by common rules.

One pondered on the life of man,
His hopes, his ending, and began
To rate the Market's sordid war
As something scarce worth living for.

'I'll brace to higher aims,' said he,
'I'll further Truth and Purity;
Thereby to mend the mortal lot
And sweeten sorrow. Thrive I not,

'Winning their hearts, my kind will give
Enough that I may lowly live,
And house my Love in some dim dell,
For pleasing them and theirs so well.'

Idly attired, with features wan,
In secret swift he laboured on:
Such press of power had brought much gold
Applied to things of meaner mould.

Sometimes he wished his aims had been
To gather gains like other men;
Then thanked his God he'd traced his track
Too far for wish to drag him back.

He lookèd from his loft one day
To where his slighted garden lay;
Nettles and hemlock hid each lawn,
And every flower was starved and gone.

He fainted in his heart, whereon
He rose, and sought his plighted one,
Resolved to loose her bond withal,
Lest she should perish in his fall.

He met her with a careless air,
As though he'd ceased to find her fair,
And said: 'True love is dust to me;
I cannot kiss: I tire of thee!'

(That she might scorn him was he fain,
To put her sooner out of pain;
For incensed love breathes quick and dies,
When famished love a-lingering lies.)

Once done, his soul was so betossed,
It found no more the force it lost:
Hope was his only drink and food,
And hope extinct, decay ensued.

And, living long so closely penned,
He had not kept a single friend;
He dwindled thin as phantoms be,
And drooped to death in poverty...

Meantime his schoolmate had gone out
To join the fortune-finding rout;

He liked the winnings of the mart,
But wearied of the working part.

He turned to seek a privy lair,
Neglecting note of garb and hair,
And day by day reclined and thought
How he might live by doing nought.

'I plan a valued scheme,' he said
To some. 'But lend me of your bread,
And when the vast result looms nigh,
In profit you shall stand as I.'

Yet they took counsel to restrain
Their kindness till they saw the gain;
And, since his substance now had run,
He rose to do what might be done.

He went unto his Love by night,
And said: 'My Love, I faint in fight:
Deserving as thou dost a crown,
My cares shall never drag thee down.'

(He had descried a maid whose line
Would hand her on much corn and wine,
And held her far in worth above
One who could only pray and love.)

But this Fair read him; whence he failed
To do the deed so blithely hailed;
He saw his projects wholly marred,
And gloom and want oppressed him hard;

Till, living to so mean an end,
Whereby he'd lost his every friend,
He perished in a pauper sty,
His mate the dying pauper nigh.

And moralists, reflecting, said,
As 'dust to dust' in burial read
Was echoed from each coffin-lid,
'These men were like in all they did.'

1866

Lines

Spoken by Miss Ada Rehan at the Lyceum Theatre, July 23, 1890,
at a performance on behalf of Lady Jeune's Holiday Fund for City Children.

Before we part to alien thoughts and aims,
Permit the one brief word the occasion claims:
– When mumming and grave projects are allied,
Perhaps an Epilogue is justified.

Our under-purpose has, in truth, to-day
Commanded most our musings; least the play:
A purpose futile but for your good-will
Swiftly responsive to the cry of ill:
A purpose all too limited! – to aid
Frail human flowerets, sicklied by the shade,
In winning some short spell of upland breeze,
Or strengthening sunlight on the level leas.

Who has not marked, where the full cheek should be,
Incipient lines of lank flaccidity,
Lymphatic pallor where the pink should glow,
And where the throb of transport, pulses low? –
Most tragical of shapes from Pole to Line,
O wondering child, unwitting Time's design,
Why should Art add to Nature's quandary,
And worsen ill by thus immuring thee?
– That races do despite unto their own,
That Might supernal do indeed condone
Wrongs individual for the general ease,
Instance the proof in victims such as these.

135

Launched into thoroughfares too thronged before,
Mothered by those whose protest is 'No more!'
Vitalised without option: who shall say
That did Life hang on choosing --Yea or Nay –
They had not scorned it with such penalty,
And nothingness implored of Destiny?

And yet behind the horizon smile serene
The down, the cornland, and the stretching green –
Space – the child's heaven: scenes which at least ensure
Some palliative for ill they cannot cure.

Dear friends – now moved by this poor show of ours
To make your own long joy in buds and bowers
For one brief while the joy of infant eyes,
Changing their urban murk to paradise –
You have our thanks! – may your reward include
More than our thanks, far more: their gratitude.

'I Look into my Glass'

I look into my glass,
And view my wasting skin,
And say, 'Would God it came to pass
My heart had shrunk as thin!'

For then, I, undistrest
By hearts grown cold to me,
Could lonely wait my endless rest
With equanimity.

But Time, to make me grieve;
Part steals, lets part abide;
And shakes this fragile frame at eve
With throbbings of noontide.

NOTES

1. Napoleon Bonaparte (1769–1821), French general and emperor (1804–15).

2. Novel by Hardy, set during the Napoleonic wars.

3. Reference to the Peninsular War (1808–14), one of the major conflicts of the Napoleonic wars.

4. One-act play written by Hardy in 1892.

5. Short story by Hardy, first published in *Longman's Magazine*.

6. The River Froom/Frome.

7. Michel Ney, duc d'Elchingen (1769–1815), French marshal; Auguste de Marmont, duc de Ragusa, (1774–1852), French general and nobleman.

8. Comte Henri Gratien Bertrand, (1773–1844), French general who shared Napoleon's banishment to Elba; Claude Victor-Perrin, duc de Belluno (1764–1841), marshal of France; Pierre Augereau, duc de Castiglione (1757–1816), French soldier, promoted marshal in 1804; Prince Józef Poniatowski (1763–1813), Polish general who fought with Napoleon in his Russian campaign, and again at Leipzig; Jacques Bernard Law, marquis de Lauriston (1768–1828), French soldier and diplomat.

9. Jacques MacDonald, Duke of Taranto (1765–1840), French soldier of Scottish descent.

10. 'If Marshall Grouchy had been reached by the officer whom Napoleon had sent to him at ten o'clock the previous evening, the whole problem would have vanished. But this officer had not got to his destination, as the Marshall never stopped claiming all his life long, and we have to believe him, for otherwise he would have had no reason to hesitate. Had this officer been captured? Had he gone over to the enemy? This has never been discovered.' (French)

11. Charles William Ferdinand, duke of Brunswick-Lüneburg, (1735–1806), Prussian field marshal.

12. Emmanuel, Marquis de Grouchy (1766–1847), French general and marshal.

13. Gebhard Leberecht von Blücher (1742–1819), Prussian field marshal who defeated Napoleon at Leipzig.

14. Sir John Ormsby Vandeleur (1763–1849), British soldier who took command of the British cavalry at Waterloo; Richard Hussey Vivian, (1775–1842), British cavalry leader; Sir Peregrine Maitland (1777– 1854), British soldier who served with distinction at Waterloo; Sir James Kempt (1764–1854), British general.

15. Jean-Baptiste Drouet, Comte d'Erlon (1765–1844), French commander at Waterloo; Louis Friant (1758–1829), French general; Ney, see note 7 above.

16. The men named in this stanza and the preceding three all fought, and most were wounded and killed, at Waterloo.

17. Three rivers in Somerset.

18. 1887 novel by Hardy.

GLOSSARY

blee: *colour, complexion*
caddle: *disorder, trouble,*
    disturbance
chiel: *man, fellow*
codlin-tree: *apple tree*
coll: *embrace, hug*
dorp: *hamlet*
emprise: *undertaking*
eyne: *eyes*
fauss'bray: *faussebraie –*
    artificial mound made
    in front of a rampart
gallied: *frightened*
grintern: *granary bin*
leaze: *pasture, common*
lewth: *warmth, shelter*
linhay: *shed or farm building*
mixens: *dunghills, compost*
nimb: *nimbus, halo*
prow: *good, worthy, valiant*
shrammed: *numbed with*
    cold
slat: *a slap, sharp blow*
slent: *split, cleave; tear*
snock: *a knock, blow*
spatters: *short for spatter-*
    dashes, long gaiters
    worn to keep trousers
    or stockings clean

stillicide: *the falling of water*
    in drops
tallet: *hayloft*
tardle: *tangle, entanglement*
touse: *shake about*
tranter: *someone who buys up*
    goods to sell on elsewhere
unshent: *unashamed;*
    undamaged
unweeting: *unknowing*
vamped: *tramped, trudged*
vlanker: *a spark of fire*

Thomas Hardy was born in Dorset in 1840, the son of a stone-mason. From an early age he developed a love for music – his father in fact taught him the violin – and his mother instilled in him an interest in books and the countryside. A sickly child, Hardy did not attend school until the age of eight when he was sent to the county school in Dorchester. From there he was articled to a local architect, and then moved to London to work for Arthur Blomfield, the prominent architect. His continuing ill-health, however, forced him to return to Dorset.

In 1868, Hardy met Emma Gifford, who was later to become his wife. She encouraged him greatly in his writing, and his first published novel, *Desperate Remedies*, appeared in 1871. It met with very little success. However, *Under the Greenwood Tree*, published the following year, was widely read and brought Hardy popular acclaim. This early work, like much of his writing, incorporated many Dorset places into a fictional plot. *Under the Greenwood Tree* was followed by *A Pair of Blue Eyes* (1873), a serialised work, and *Far From the Madding Crowd* (1874) – the novel that finally allowed Hardy to leave architecture and write full time.

Hardy and his wife moved around during the next few years, based mainly in Dorset but also living for a short while in London. They finally settled in Dorchester in 1887, in a house that Hardy himself had designed, and it was here that he penned *The Mayor of Casterbridge* (1886), *The Woodlanders* (1887) and, perhaps his best-loved work, *Tess of the D'Urbervilles* (1891). *Tess* aroused considerable interest, but his next work, *Jude the Obscure* (1895), provoked a sea of controversy for its unorthodox treatment of marriage. Hardy was greatly surprised – and dismayed – by this reaction, and turned away from fiction, choosing instead to focus on poetry. He produced a number of volumes, including the famous *Wessex Poems* (1898).

Emma Hardy died in 1912, and Hardy was immediately stricken with grief and remorse. He poured out his feelings in his poetry, thereby producing some of the most moving lines he ever wrote. He was married again in 1914 – to Florence Dugdale, his secretary since 1912 – and the two of them remained in Dorchester until Hardy's death in 1928. He was buried in Poet's Corner in Westminster Abbey, although, in accordance with his wishes, his heart was placed alongside Emma's grave in Stinsford churchyard.

SELECTED TITLES FROM HESPERUS PRESS

Author	Title	Foreword writer
Louisa May Alcott	*Behind a Mask*	Doris Lessing
Dante Alighieri	*New Life*	Louis de Bernières
Dante Alighieri	*The Divine Comedy: Inferno*	Ian Thomson
Edmondo de Amicis	*Constantinople*	Umberto Eco
Pietro Aretino	*The School of Whoredom*	Paul Bailey
Jane Austen	*Lesley Castle*	Zoë Heller
Jane Austen	*Love and Friendship*	Fay Weldon
Charles Baudelaire	*On Wine and Hashish*	Margaret Drabble
Giovanni Boccaccio	*Life of Dante*	A.N. Wilson
Charlotte Brontë	*The Green Dwarf*	Libby Purves
Charlotte Brontë	*The Secret*	Salley Vickers
Charlotte Brontë	*The Spell*	Nicola Barker
Emily Brontë	*Poems of Solitude*	Helen Dunmore
Giacomo Casanova	*The Duel*	Tim Parks
Miguel de Cervantes	*The Dialogue of the Dogs*	Ben Okri
Geoffrey Chaucer	*The Parliament of Birds*	
Anton Chekhov	*The Story of a Nobody*	Louis de Bernières
Anton Chekhov	*Three Years*	William Fiennes
Wilkie Collins	*A Rogue's Life*	Peter Ackroyd
Wilkie Collins	*Who Killed Zebedee?*	Martin Jarvis
William Congreve	*Incognita*	Peter Ackroyd
Joseph Conrad	*Heart of Darkness*	A.N. Wilson
Joseph Conrad	*The Return*	Colm Tóibín
James Fenimore Cooper	*Autobiography of a Pocket Handkerchief*	Ruth Scurr
Daniel Defoe	*The King of Pirates*	Peter Ackroyd
Charles Dickens	*The Haunted House*	Peter Ackroyd
Charles Dickens	*Mrs Lirriper*	Philip Hensher
Charles Dickens	*Mugby Junction*	Robert Macfarlane

Charles Dickens	*The Wreck of the Golden Mary*	Simon Callow
Emily Dickinson	*The Single Hound*	Andrew Motion
Fyodor Dostoevsky	*The Double*	Jeremy Dyson
Fyodor Dostoevsky	*The Gambler*	Jonathan Franzen
Fyodor Dostoevsky	*Notes from the Underground*	Will Self
Fyodor Dostoevsky	*Poor People*	Charlotte Hobson
Arthur Conan Doyle	*The Tragedy of the Korosko*	Tony Robinson
Alexandre Dumas	*Captain Pamphile*	Tony Robinson
George Eliot	*Mr Gilfil's Love Story*	Kirsty Gunn
J. Meade Falkner	*The Lost Stradivarius*	Tom Paulin
Henry Fielding	*Jonathan Wild the Great*	Peter Ackroyd
Gustave Flaubert	*Memoirs of a Madman*	Germaine Greer
Gustave Flaubert	*November*	Nadine Gordimer
E.M. Forster	*Arctic Summer*	Anita Desai
Elizabeth Gaskell	*Lois the Witch*	Jenny Uglow
Theophile Gautier	*The Jinx*	Gilbert Adair
André Gide	*Theseus*	
Johann Wolfgang von Goethe	*The Man of Fifty*	A.S. Byatt
Nikolai Gogol	*The Squabble*	Patrick McCabe
Thomas Hardy	*Fellow-Townsmen*	Emma Tennant
Nathaniel Hawthorne	*Rappaccini's Daughter*	Simon Schama
Victor Hugo	*The Last Day of a Condemned Man*	Libby Purves
Henry James	*In the Cage*	Libby Purves
John Keats	*Fugitive Poems*	Andrew Motion
D.H. Lawrence	*Daughters of the Vicar*	Anita Desai
D.H. Lawrence	*The Fox*	Doris Lessing
Giacomo Leopardi	*Thoughts*	Edoardo Albinati
Mikhail Lermontov	*A Hero of Our Time*	Doris Lessing

Leo Tolstoy	*Hadji Murat*	Colm Tóibín
Ivan Turgenev	*Faust*	Simon Callow
Mark Twain	*The Diary of Adam and Eve*	John Updike
Jules Verne	*A Fantasy of Dr Ox*	Gilbert Adair
Leonardo da Vinci	*Prophecies*	Eraldo Affinati
Edith Wharton	*Sanctuary*	William Fiennes
Edith Wharton	*The Touchstone*	Salley Vickers
Oscar Wilde	*The Portrait of Mr W.H.*	Peter Ackroyd
Virginia Woolf	*Carlyle's House and Other Sketches*	Doris Lessing
Virginia Woolf	*Monday or Tuesday*	Scarlett Thomas
Virginia Woolf, Vanessa Bell with Thoby Stephen	*Hyde Park Gate News*	Hermione Lee
Emile Zola	*The Dream*	Tim Parks
Emile Zola	*For a Night of Love*	A.N. Wilson